NO KIDDING, GOD, WHERE ARE YOU?

by Lou Ruoff

Resource Publications, Inc.
160 E. Virginia St. #290
San Jose, CA 95112

Editorial director: Kenneth Guentert
Production editor: Elizabeth J. Asborno
Book cover design and production: Andrew Wong
Editorial assistant: Linda D'Angelo

Library of Congress Cataloging in Publication Data

Ruoff, Lou, 1946-
   No kidding, God, where are you? / Lou Ruoff.
      p.   cm.
   ISBN 0-89390-141-5
   1. Bible. N.T. Gospels—Liturgical lessons, English—Meditations.
2. Jesus Christ—Parables—Meditations. 3. Parables—Paraphrases, tales, etc. I. Title.
BS2565.R86 1989
242—dc19   88-34043

97 96 95 94 93 | 7 6 5 4 3

One half of royalties received from this book will be given by the author to Freedom House (Richmond, Virginia), an organization that provides food and shelter to street people.

Peace

Lou Rawls

This book is dedicated to my deceased friend Michael and his children, Michele Leigh and Michael IV.

"Do not let your hearts be troubled. You have faith in God; have faith also in me. In my Father's house there are many dwelling places. If there were not, would I have told you that I am going to prepare a place for you? And if I go and prepare a place for you, I will come back again and take you to myself, so that where I am you also may be" (Jn 14:1-3 NAB).

AN ACT OF TRUST

When you can tell me your story, and I can bring to it my own feelings, my own past, my own peculiar way of seeing things, then—your story can speak to where I live.
I may change it around a bit in the process.
If you can accept my doing, then your story becomes a precious gift to me, and I make it truly my own.
Sharing a story is an act of trust.

Ralph Milton
(From an article published in *Alive Now* entitled "The Gift of Story." Used with permission.)

Contents

Foreword

Dear Reader:

The story of God's participation in our lives is told through the stories of people. The Old and New Testaments give witness to God's intervention through the lives of His people. In story form God reveals himself as a gracious and loving God.

Stories do not end with the death of the last apostle. Faith continues through the lives of others. Father Lou Ruoff has captured the value of storytelling. He does so through his own life experiences which have led him to a deeper appreciation of God in his own life.

These stories should be an inspiration to others. The stories will help the reader to come in contact with his or her experiences. The book will encourage the reader to share faith stories with others.

This book should prove an inspiration to many who share together the journey of faith.

Sincerely yours in Christ,

Walter F. Sullivan
Bishop of Richmond, Virginia

Acknowledgments

One day as I was sharing a story or two with the parish secretary, she suggested that I write a book. I responded, "Huh?" The more I thought, the more it sounded plausible that a book of parables relating to my experiences of life and Jesus/God was not out of the question. My thanks to that secretary and to all church secretaries.

And thank you, Emily, for being a teacher to me. A dedicated MRE to the Church she serves well!

Special thanks to Bishop Walter F. Sullivan, Ordinary of Richmond, for his support of my ministry to God's people.

I want to thank all the priests with whom I served. I have learned from each of you. I want to especially thank Michael Schmied, P. Francis Quinn, Fred Cwiekowski, Denis O'Callaghan (d), Gil Weil, John McGinley, Lloyd Stephenson, John Lyle, Sean Winters, and John Adams for their encouragement and support.

I want to thank my closest friends who have shared the good times as well as the bad times with me. They have nourished me with their understanding and *love!*

Vince Malone & Family,
Carl Fierimonte & Family,
John Grugan & Family,
Fred Schrandt,
Bob Meany,
Carl Hocke,
Mary Ann Allen,
Karen Grant,
Sandy Dice Adkins,
John Wozniak.

And a final thanks to the people of God from the following parishes:

St. Elizabeth Parish, Richmond, VA
St. Joseph Parish, Petersburg, VA
Holy Comforter Parish, Charlottesville, VA
Our Lady of Perpetual Help Parish,
Salem, VA

for all their love and support!

Even with all kinds of love and encouragement, I felt many times that these parables/stories were not good enough for publication. Then I traveled to the land of Benjamin Franklin and my birth to seek out an authoritative opinion. I met with Rev. Gerald Sloyan, who said they were good enough. Thank you, Gerald! And thank you, Virginia.

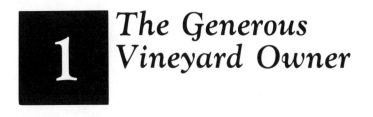 The Generous Vineyard Owner

---

25th Sunday of Ordinary Time (A)   Matthew 20:1-16

Recently a man who was a model of discipleship died. He was a prayerful person, always doing acts for others. He was faithful to his marriage commitment and helped rear two fine children. He worked at the same company for thirty-five years as general manager, and he always acted with the highest regard for ethics. He was much involved in civic and church activities, so that those less fortunate might benefit. He acted courageously in private life and did not allow weaknesses to interfere with his life. As was said, he was a model creature.

On his deathbed, when the moment came for him to meet his Maker, it was reported that a faint smile crossed his face—for he was to receive his eternal reward.

At the moment of death, the man was welcomed into heaven by St. Peter. He was told the "dos" and "don'ts." The man was also told that God would personally interview him as soon as time allowed, but, in the meantime, he was invited to take a walk through the endless streets of heaven.

It so happened that this man seemed to notice seven of the most notorious people of the twentieth century; they were having a meeting of sorts. The seven were eating and drinking amid much lively conversation that seemed friendly enough. The man became indignant and out-raged—even to the point of anger. "This isn't the way it's supposed to be! They should all be suffering in hell!" he said to himself and then out loud.

Finally the man's interview with God came, and he con-fronted God with a barrage of questions. God's love for this man could be seen instantly, and God made no fur-ther attempts to reassure love—heaven was God's love for the man.

Somehow the news made its way down to earth—no one really knows how—but it upset many good and righteous people. The people were fuming, so much so that there was a request for God to be questioned by all humanity about this whole incident. And God *agreed*!

God came amid the greatest flock of newspaper people in history. Cameras from every part of the globe were there. Every radio and television station carried this "news con-ference" live! Every inch of space was crowded with
>   the curious,
>   the good,
>   the bad,
>   the young,
>   the old,
>   the sick,
>   the faithful, and
>   the unbelievers.

When it was time for the first question, silence reigned supreme. An American reporter opened the conference with this question, "Eternal One, will you comment on the report that

> Hitler,
> Capone,
> Stalin,
> Lenin,
> Mao Tse-Tung,
> Mussolini, and
> Kaiser Wilhelm

are all in heaven?

The Lord said, "No Comment."

A German reporter stood up next and asked, "Could you comment, Creator, on the lives each of these men lived while on earth?"

The Lord said, "No Comment."

With that, a Chinese reporter inquired, "Wise One, these men, collectively speaking, have been responsible for the destruction of tens of millions of lives—do you condone their actions?"

Again, "No Comment," said God.

An Italian reporter then pursued, "Absolute One, if these men are indeed in heaven, and are saved, think of the effort the righteous have put into their lives in their lifetime; they have kept to the straight and narrow, only to see sinners admitted to paradise—it seems unfair. Any comment, Spirit?"

God said, "No Comment."

Finally, a Russian reporter demanded, "None of them, Infinite One, took you seriously. In fact, most of them denied you even existed. How can you even recognize them, Blessed One?"

God responded,
> "I AM the Maker of love, who is generous
> with my love.
> I AM free to do as I please with my love
> and forgiveness—
> AM I not? Could it be you are jealous be-
> cause I AM so generous?"

With that, the news conference ended.

ॐ

This story is intentionally embellished to make a two-fold point:

1) no one has to merit God's love—it is given to everyone; nor does anyone have a claim to God's forgiveness. Thus, no one earns heaven. It is, again, God's ultimate mercy, which can neither be analyzed nor defined.

2) each of us must stand alone before God—and personally, I stand before God in complete humbleness, knowing I am never deserving of forgiveness but always needing God's mercy. Can any of us stand before God without divine mercy?

2 *The Samaritan at the Well*

3rd Sunday of Lent (A)   **John 4:1-42**

Have you ever noticed the world is full of boundaries? Boundaries are those things that seem to separate one area of land from another; those obstacles that separate people from other people; those hindrances that create the *we's* and the *they's*.

Just the other day, while riding in my car across the state, what was beautifully illustrated to me was the natural demarcation of land, where a particular territory ended and where another space began. These natural demarcations abound in their own attractiveness and mystery:

> the picturesque mountains,
> the giant slopes,
> the massive gullies,
> rock formations,
> soil erosion,
> rivers,
> lakes, and
> trees.

The separation of territories has many positive aspects about it. Animals, for example, will use a certain territory as their personal space, instinctively surviving their common predators while in the wilds of the wilderness.

While I was eating my lunch on such a day at a nearby lake, I observed some beavers using the natural boundary of water not only as a means of survival but as a way to secure for them their own habitat as well.

At the same time, I was attentive to the multitude of human-made boundaries covering the vast landscape. These human boundaries seemed to be giving a variety of messages to the masses of folks who came in contact with these separations.

The most common of all human boundaries is the fence. A fence sends a message to an individual who happens to be in the same general area; but also each fence has its own distinctive personality.

Some fences are pleasant and inviting, whereas others are callous and threatening—even harmful.

The most amicable of all fences is the picket fence. The picket fence has no pretense about itself. It is a fence with no hidden agenda; we see what we see. The picket fence is quite friendly, likes to smile a lot, and loves company. The strength of this fence is that it rallies people together and enables neighborhoods to communicate and work in unison for the common good of all.

Another common boundary is the split rail fence, which dates back to early America. This fence is rich in history, tradition, and wealth. Of all fences, the split rail fence is the most sophisticated because it takes pride in its hospitality, appreciative of visitors who come to view the beauty of the house it surrounds.

Most of the remaining fences have chores to accomplish. The snow fence holds the drifts in place while the rope fence is occupied with crowd control. The framed chain-link fence is committed to the protection of people and property as much as the dedicated guard-rail fence on the nation's highways. The chicken coop fence has saved a many would-be wanderer.

The most threatening fences are the concrete slab and the barbed wire fence. The concrete slab is dangerous. The message it sends is "don't come near or you'll get hurt." We know pointedly we are not welcome. People feel uneasy and uncomfortable by the very presence of the concrete slab.

Even more dangerous is the barbed wire fence. Unlike the concrete slab, the barbed wire fence is deceiving. The message given, "come near me if you dare," allows for a certain amount of human misjudgment. This fence is most feared because, though one may see through its opening and see things and people that seem to offer hope, it usually courts ultimate tragedy. People are duped because they often become careless and intrude onto the space forbidden by the barbed wire. The fence reacts viciously when this occurs,
> cutting,
> destroying,
> scarring for life.

Barbed wire fences have been around for a good period of time. Barbed wire fences were erected at the death camps of Auschwitz and Buchenwald, and a barbed wire fence is currently splitting the cities of East and West Berlin. Barbed wire fences have segregated the Navajo and Apache people from other Americans, and barbed wire fences encompass many prisons the world over.

One injustice during the time of Jesus was the invisible barbed wire that encircled the entire Samaritan community. Samaritans were outlawed by the Jewish people because of their mixed, pagan blood. Thus the Samaritans were disfranchised people: ostracized and branded, surrounded by enmity and ill will. And no wonder an air of antagonism arose when Jesus asked for water from the Samaritan women. Jesus, with his every word, penetrated and cut through the wire of inequality. The woman became free from the scars of hatred and oppression because of a Jew who wouldn't tolerate a symbol of separation.

Many strides have been made to tear down symbols that divided people in the last twenty-five years or so. From race to religion, the barriers have fallen!

As I am looking out from our modern Catholic church on this bright Sunday morning, I can see our neighboring Baptist church—and I can see a *barbed wire fence separating our two churches.*

Covenant

1st Sunday of Lent (B)   Genesis 9:8-15; Mark 1:12-15

Good morning, my name is—er, was—*Philadelphia Bulletin.*

I am no longer alive.

That is, I'm no longer with you on earth.

I am where all good newspapers go when they are called by their Maker. I didn't want to go, but, being an obedient public servant, I went when called.

On April 12, 1847, in the "city of brotherly love," in a house as tiny as the street it stood on (108 S. 3rd St.), I was born as an experiment. Those early years were rough, but I managed to sell enough papers that at the age of eighteen I moved into larger quarters at 607 Chestnut Street. My great reputation flourished during the period from 1895-1935, when my circulation grew from 33,625 to 300,000-plus. From 612 Chestnut Street I moved in 1908 to the most modern newspaper plant of my day at Filbert and Juniper Sts. After forty-seven years at that location, I moved to my final address at 30th and Market Sts. In my heydays of the forties and fifties, my circulation rose astronomically, which placed me among the best newspapers in the country. I enjoyed my career immensely, but my health gave way to a chronic illness during the seventies until I died January 29, 1982, at the age of 134.

Through good and bad times, generations of Philadelphians welcomed me into their homes as a friend—almost as a member of the family. And when I rolled off the presses for the last time, it was in many respects the death of a covenant. Yes, covenant.

The covenant established by me (and my parents) to my readers was that I would offer all the news without bias and report the news with candor, acuracy, and dispatch.

And because I entered a home as a family member, that was a privilege I honored, and I would never allow myself to be unfaithful to my "mission statement." In return, my readers would oblige by paying my rent to secure my permanent existence.

As years passed that covenant grew and matured. It was obvious to everyone that a bond existed between myself and the public—a covenant based on respect and love.

Stories of covenant are nothing new with me; I reported many of them. Some covenant stories are without parallel or comparison, and I can only marvel at them in awe. The flood story in Genesis and the desert story in Mark are two noteworthy examples.

In the Genesis story, flood waters destroy the world as a sign that the bond apparently has been broken between God and the "chosen people." The "chosen people" failed to live according to the standard given them, thus closing shop to God's Covenant. The earth is destroyed just like the fabric of a major city when it loses an honored newspaper.

In Mark's story, the Spirit of the Lord leads Jesus to the desert. Jesus is put to the test while alone among the beasts of the wilderness. Apparently Jesus had to confront the great adversary in the loneliness of his journey.

The paradoxical similarity of both accounts is the reassurance that God's Covenant lives.

In the flood event, the awesome love of God prevails despite the destruction of the earth. Out of that destruction, God forms a new Covenant, something even a distinguished newspaper cannot do. The New Covenant is not just with a nation, but with the whole of humankind forever. All are invited to partake in this new beginning; in fact, a new creation in which Noah is seen as the "new Adam." Moreover, the only condition established is from the Lord Yahweh: "I will establish my Covenant with you, that never again shall all bodily creatures be destroyed."

The lesson of the desert account is that good will ultimately triumph. God can never abandon us. Though, like Jesus, people will be tempted and deception will be ever around, God will never allow people's words, when confronted with evil, to dribble like my newsprint when exposed to rain. Jesus is seen as the fullness of God in our lives: the total revelation of spirit and love.

This Covenant from God is for all; it is unconditional:
>no one has to earn God's love—it is given;
>no one has to merit God's graces—it is free;
>no one has to compete for God's mercy—it is there.

The God who conveys Covenant to all humankind acts
yet in a very personal sense. God
> is God to all people;
> is a God
>> who touches people,
>> who feels for people,
>> who acts with people,

and they are urged to call upon God in the most personal
of terms.

Covenant also means faith in the wonders of God. Not
only does God love but God redeems; He is a God who
promises salvation through Jesus.

During the next six weeks, the entire community is called
to self-reflection, a period of seeing where the community
is and where the community intends to go. We approach
a period of refocusing goals, a period of soul searching to
seek the Almighty, who has established the path by the
great Covenant.

I am dead, never to form a bond again with my readers.
But God lives; Covenant lives forever.

The *Philadelphia Bulletin* is nowhere to be found; thus the
news is stilled. Yet God can be found—for God has given
us *good news* that can never be stilled!

The Vine and Branches

5th Sunday of Easter (B)   John 15:1-8

When I was younger, say about nine years old, I left the orphanage to be placed in a foster home. In that foster house my personhood was not truly accepted. I felt I was just an addition to the household, another piece of furniture, if you will. Love for me was not expressed either verbally or actively. Although I could neither intelligently nor adequately express myself then, I somehow recognized the feelings within me.

After several months at the foster house, I ran away. I wandered the streets for an endless period of time, going absolutely nowhere. All I thought was, "Where do I belong?"

Soon I found a patch of land that had a delightful pond right smack in the middle of it! I remember lying by the pond and watching the sparkling water moving ever so gracefully. I readied myself for a peaceful nap when I noticed a rather small and seemingly displaced oak tree, about three times my height. It overshadowed me. As I was staring at this frail ornament of nature, I was taken back to earlier days when I felt I knew a much older oak tree well enough to converse with. I guessed that big oak tree was the father of the small oak tree, because it was

so big,

so huge,

so magnificent

as it stood in all the glory some hundred feet up in the sky. It was the most gigantic tree I had ever laid eyes on! It was also the most approachable.

The big oak tree and I shared many secrets together. I would tell the big oak tree all my thoughts and concerns. We had such a great and unique relationship; it brought us close; it brought us to understanding. We had a sense of belonging together.

All these thoughts were going through my mind when I was rudely awakened by the raindrops falling from the clouds. I had fallen asleep for a few hours and when awakened, the night had arrived—and I knew I had to go somewhere. Suddenly, I heard a whisper coming from the small oak tree, "Where do I belong?" I didn't know what to say; I was caught by surprise.

My search continued. I arrived at a nearby state police barracks seeking

a haven,

a refuge.

I asked the officer in charge to take me to where I belonged. After telling the officer my story and the story of the small oak tree, he assured me everything would be alright. That night I slept at the barracks, fully contented that all would be well the next day.

Where I belonged was

where I was cared for,

where I was well dressed,

where I was fed abundantly,

where I had a warm place to rest my head,
where my coughs and sniffles were taken
  seriously,
where my spiritual and intellectual needs
  were met,
where love was expressed in countless
  ways.

The next day's ride back to the orphanage, my home, was most exciting. Once back, I resumed my unique relationship with the big oak tree. I told the big oak tree all that I had seen, especially the little oak tree. I experienced a newfound appreciation for this tree that had blessed me with its gifts of time and shade for so many years without ever asking anything in return.

A month later, I was told that I had a visitor. In all my years in the orphanage, I had never had a visitor. I wondered who it might be. The visitor turned out to be the officer I had sought refuge with. He told me he had a surprise for me—you're right!—it was that small oak tree! We dug a home for the small oak tree right next to the big oak tree. I promised the officer that I would take care of both oak trees.

Months later I realized two astonishing facts: my small oak tree was not really an oak tree; in actuality, it was an ordinary apple tree that gave abundant, delicious apples to *all* the youngsters in the orphanage!

Secondly, I realized that I was actually bringing to completion the fullness of God's many gifts by caring for my small oak—oops, apple—tree, which was entrusted to us all; I was a co-creator, if you will.

The officer
>   who came to see,
> .   who helped me plant,
>   who gave meaning to it all—
>   who was he?
Perhaps you can answer that question? I already know.

The Love of God

6th Sunday of Easter (B)   **John 15:9-17**

How many of us have ever played, even once, hopscotch? Almost everyone has played this rather simple game. Simple, yes; but it also has a very profound quality to it.

Let me take a few minutes to explain how I used to play when I was younger. There are eight blocks to this game, and the object is to throw your marker, say a pebble, on a particular block as you go up and down the board without losing your balance nor touching a dividing line. More specifically, when you throw a pebble on, say the first block, you hop with one leg past the first three blocks without touching a line. Both of your feet must land, separately, on the 4th and 5th blocks, then continue on to block six with, again, one foot. Blocks 7 and 8 are tricky, because as you land your feet separately on these two blocks, you then turn your body around to begin the journey back to the initial first block. Once successfully completing the first try, the same format is continued until you have successfully completed throwing the pebble on all the individual blocks.

Well, the game of life and our relationship to God is similar to playing hopscotch. There are many roadblocks/crises in our lives that threaten our relationship with God and with one another. These blocks represent various

> situations,
> threats, and
> quagmires.

The pebble is our willingness to live life each and everyday. It represents decisions we are called to make. Many of them will be tough decisions.

The first block is the most simple, the most important, the most critical. And it is the least understood. The first block tells us *God loves us*. Most of us really pay no mind to that, except to say, "God is to me what I want God to be." In other words, we measure God for the suit instead of allowing the Maker to rightly be the tailor. It is a very simple block, but because of our misconceptions, many of us continue the game shouldering a heavy burden that adds suspense to the game.

The second block is again simple, but nonetheless often misunderstood. The second block is *gift:* The gift of life in all its forms. I am a gift to everyone, and everyone is a gift to me. We don't always view or remember this formula, especially when the gift commits a violent act against another human gift. In turn, we hate or even kill that gift. The lesson to be learned is bungled, which sets the stage for future human conduct. We are sure to lose our balance if we continue to ignore people as gift.

The third block is *family*. Again it is simple but now the burden begins to show: if *God* is misunderstood and if *gift* is ignored, the rippling effect on a family will be a tremendous strain because all our actions in the outside world are determined, in one way or another, by how we handle family disputes and problems. Family is relationship in its highest form and it will take hard work and a good amount of patience to perfect it. If we can master the first three blocks, the rest of the way can be a breeze.

The fourth and fifth blocks should be approached carefully. These two blocks are *commitment* and *prayer*. This is the first time two feet can land at the same time, one foot in two different blocks. A mature way of life will require our heart and mind to be totally involved in commitment to prayer, a committed prayer life, if you will. I can guarantee you, but Jesus said it before me, if one takes these two blocks seriously, balance can be achieved even though there may have been a shaky start. If not, the rest of the way will be a very trying experience indeed.

The sixth block is the hardest. If we are ever going to lose our balance, this block will be the cause. This block represents *values*, or the lack of them. In Jesus' day, they were called "false gods"—that is to say, gods that come before our God. These gods, whose names are

> Greed,
> Lust, and
> Selfishness,

are by themselves not life-threatening. But if our journey up to this point has been lacking, then these gods are surely detrimental, and our game is doomed.

The seventh and eighth blocks are our saving grace. When approaching these, we are beginning to feel our helplessness: we are tired and exhausted, yet we have to make a reversal and head back to the first block—and if you remember, it's name is *God loves us. Jesus Christ* is the name of the seventh and eighth blocks. Jesus will

> seek,
> lead, and
> guide

us back to the *God who loves us.*

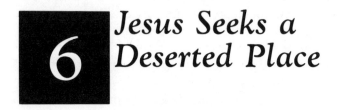

6 Jesus Seeks a Deserted Place

16th Sunday of Ordinary Time (B)   **Mark 6:30-34**

Jesus wanted to go to a deserted place to pray alone
        in silence,
        with silence.

In silence. Alone. By Himself.

In silence.

Silence:

        it doesn't make a sound;
        it can be good, it can be bad.

Silence:

        it cannot be found; it cannot be felt;
        it cannot be seen. It is just there.

Silence:

        it gives comfort, it can also be devastating;
        it was here before the world began;
        it will be here when the world ends.

Silence:

> it is where God can be found;
> that is why Jesus sought out a place
> to be with silence,
> in silence.

God created the seed of silence first

> and after many eons,
> God created a big bang that started the
> activity of the world
> but no one was around to hear it.

Silence:

> it settled to being only a bit player
> in the world of creation
> and movement.

There appeared

> the Sun,
> the stars,
> the moon;
> light was shining everywhere.

There was the sound of the wind against the redwoods,
and the forest had the noise of

> the birds,
> the elephants
> and even the crickets!

They added more life to a less silent world.

God was pleased with all the noise, but God wanted
something more. God wanted noise and silence to be
compatible, so God created the human family.

At first humans were silent, then groans were heard, then
after many eons

> the human family began chipping the clay
>   and the stones;
> the human family formulated hundreds
>   of languages that brought into the
>   world a lot of noise.

Noise:

> it can be inspiring, it can be chaotic;
> it can be powerful, it can be deafening.

Noise:

> it can bring understanding, but usually it
> brings misunderstanding;
> it can bring peace, but usually it brings
> war.

When Jesus was here he heard all the noises the human
family had to offer. They were

> voices of discontent, of disunity;
> voices of contempt and power.

Voices of joy and happiness that were once contagious
were overwhelmed by the voices of

> confusion,
> anxiety, and
> despair.

Jesus heard the voices throughout the land; it was
paralyzing. He wanted to show the human family the way
to reach his "Abba."

Jesus took his disciples to a desolate place in the hush of
the night. When they arrived there, Jesus told the disciples,

> "be still, be silent...listen, your God is
> speaking to you."

The disciples were in awe.

The disciples shared their experience of silence with the
world. The human family was eager to hear—but they
heard their own voices instead.

The human family chose to hear their own voices instead
of silence:

> a mistake,
> a blunder!

Hundreds of year later the human family was still satisfied with the voices of their own history: the voices
> of deception,
> of crusades,
> of revolutions,
> of explosions,
> of war.

And so today the human family has invested their lives in
the voices of alien tongues. The human family has invested their lives in the voices of bombs. They got their
money's worth
> in Antwerp,
> in Warsaw,
> in Berlin, and
> in Hiroshima.

The human family no longer calls them bombs. They are
called missiles today.
> Nuclear missiles to be sure.
> Nuclear to be accurate.

We live in the world today where silence is not sought; silence has become
> a stranger,
> a foreigner.

And if we continue to allow our voices to overpower us,
the human family will play God and have their own big
bang—and silence will again rule as it once did. And no
one will be around to appreciate it.

Silence:
> it doesn't make a sound;
> it can be good, it can be bad.

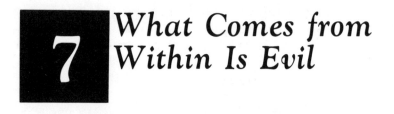

7 *What Comes from Within Is Evil*

22nd Sunday of Ordinary Time (B)   Mark 7:14-15

Have you ever noticed the many people
          who go to the beach,
          who go to the shore?

I remember going to Atlantic City and Wildwood, NJ, when I was young and having fun on the beach. Most especially, I remember building sand castles all along the beach. I was particularly good in building these sand castles—so much so that people would come from all parts of the beach and boardwalk to see all my works of art. I suppose all this architectural ability was ingrained in my bones by a big city that had a lot of tall buildings.

One noteworthy summer that comes to mind was when I wanted to share my talent with God. For some reason the winter before, while doing some Christmas shopping downtown, I marveled at one of the huge skyscrapers and wondered how on earth it was ever built. It crossed my mind that God gave us humans the ability to make all sorts of masterpieces. So that summer I decided to build my own masterpiece. I built the most gorgeous castle anyone could ever lay eyes on. The castle was complete with

> steeples,
> doors,
> windows,
> gates,
> ramps,
> a balcony,
> flag poles,
> steps,
> a porch,
> a driveway,
> a bridge leading to the castle's entrance, and of course,
> a tower.

People

> marveled at my masterpiece,
> took pictures of my masterpiece; some of them even
> offered me money to do for them the same masterpiece.

I took a swim in the ocean and it occurred to me that God has given us so many natural masterpieces. The earth is full of them. They have been here from time immemorial. We humans have a limited vocabulary for talking about the Holy One's masterpieces. Our country has been endowed and blessed with a few of them, and we call them wonders of the world:

> The Grand Canyon,
> The Grand Tetons,
> The Giant Redwood Forest,
> Natural Bridge,
> Niagara Falls,
> Mount St. Helens.

Not to be outdone by God, we humans have been hard at
work making our own masterpieces, but not to compete
with Almighty God, you understand. We make masterpieces to show The Almighty we can do some truly amaz-
ing things ourselves:
>The Pyramids of Egypt,
>The Great Wall of China,
>The Coliseum of Rome,
>The Taj Mahal of India,
>The World Trade Center,
>The Eiffel Tower,
>The Panama Canal,
>The Golden Gate Bridge,
>The Louisiana Superdome.

Understand the Lord has always been impressed by
humankind's great wonders. In fact, the other day the
Lord sat on the mighty throne and used language such as:
>marvelous,
>stupendous,
>astonishing,
>remarkable, and
>unbelievable,

to describe the admiration for our masterpieces.

But one day The Almighty inquired of all humankind:
"Your feats are beyond words, but when treating my
people, my creation, my masterpieces, you do not fare too
well. In many cases, you have taken away the dignity that
I bestowed upon every human creature. It is in that dignity that all of you are my masterpieces. But you are
depriving so many of my people, in Asia, in the Africas,
in the Americas, in fact, the world over. You are depriving, you are destroying, the heart of my masterpieces."

As I was coming back from my swim and reflection, I
noticed
>my sand castle,
>my masterpiece,
was smashed to smithereens by some careless people
walking the beach. I was fit to be tied. It was at that moment that I realized what was meant when people, by
their tongues and their actions,
>abuse,
>misuse, and
>hurt other people.

Who's the Greatest?

25th Sunday of Ordinary Time (B)   **Mark 9:30-37**

The disciples were arguing among themselves about who was

> the most essential,
> the most important, indeed,
> the greatest, serving the Master and
>   his mission.

"I am a fisherman," said one, "I go early in the morning before dawn and I'm out til dusk. I bring the food we are to eat. I am the most important!"

"I make the fish nets that enable us to catch the fish in the sea," said another, "I darn day and night. I suppose I'm the most essential."

"I build the boat and the oars that enable us to catch our haul. Without my maintenance our mission is doomed," said a third.

Others went on to say,

"I clean and cook the fish...I'm certainly critical to the cause!"

"I weave, mend, and sew our cloths. I'm needed the most!"

"I make our sandals, spend weeks carving them to perfection. I'm vital to the mission."

"I fetch the water from the sea for our baths and bring ample supply for drinking, especially when the temperature reaches 100 degrees. I can never be underrated."

"I set the Master's itinerary; being his secretary is crucial."

"I do the shopping and pay the bills. My value is undeniable."

"I do the books. My service is impeccable."

It was then that Jesus injected himself into the fray and proposed, "If anyone wishes to be first, he shall be the last and the servant of all."

You understand the disciples were eager people intoxicated with competition—and no wonder. Never before were any of them singled out for anything. Jesus was the first to explore their talents and gifts.

As you know, competition is still very rampant in our lives today, and those words of Jesus are still a lesson for us to learn. So, if anyone
>>>>>>>>>>wishes to be first,
>>>>>>>>>>wishes to be the leader, or
>>>>>>>>>>wishes to be the head honcho,
the first order of business
>>>>>>>>>>should be,
>>>>>>>>>>must be,

to discard,
to disown, and
to disavow the competitive drive we all
seem to have.

It has been said that competition
makes the ego shine;
makes the individual a much more superior and successful person;
makes the person more healthy and ener-
getic.
Even our country exhorts its virtue.

I suppose competition is fine to a point; I suppose competition is at times necessary; and, I suppose competition
can even be fun. But surely, more often than not, competition
leaves someone behind,
leaves someone stranded, and
leaves someone holding the bag.

Usually someone is left without something:
no house,
no job,
no money,
no purpose,
no dignity.

I find it interesting that Jesus also uses a child as an example in the disciples' discussion. This seems plausible
because it is when we are children that we first learn
about competition and what it can do.

When I was about nine years old, I couldn't contain
myself when the teachers told the class there would be a
spelling bee. I was excited and eager to show my
superiority. There were about sixty children in my class
and we made a circle around the classroom, all in

alphabetical order. The contest went smoothly, everyone spelling their word correctly, until I was given the word "animal" to spell. I spelled it a-n-i-n-a-l.

I was told to sit down—no
>   if's,
>   and's or
>   but's!

I was the first to drop out.

I was embarrassed, even ashamed of myself.

A pattern developed: whenever there was a spelling contest, I was always the first to be seated while others never had to feel my humiliation—they always remained standing.

To this day my spelling will never get me first into paradise. What will get me to paradise is God's love.

God doesn't care if I'm
>   the best,
>   the most important, nor
>   the greatest in anything!

All God cares about is if I am—if *we* are—serving the needs of people.

"Love God...and Your Neighbor"

31st Sunday of Ordinary Time (B)   **Mark 12:28-34**

Jesus said: "Love the Lord your God
                with all you heart,
                with all your soul,
                with all your mind,
                with all your strength,
and your neighbor as yourself."

                Excellent Sir,
                Superb Mister,
                Magnificent Master,
but how much more? How much more do you expect?

I already love God,
I love God very much; though whenever crises comes my
way and there are no immediate resolutions at hand,
                I get bent out of shape,
                I scream,
                I holler,
                I yell at everyone—even God.

And when these crises settle down and somehow resolve themselves, I know God's hand was involved because my Creator loves me very much.

I already love my family,
I love my family very much; and when I go out I make a lush of myself, and wreck the family car, and blow the family grocery money, but all I have to do is say, "I'm sorry," and they'll get over it because they love me very much.

I already love my neighbor,
I love my neighbors very much; I go so far as to write "love" on every memo I send my neighbors at the office; and when they really think I love them, I get anxious and nervous, and then I realize how much I don't, and that is when I tell them I love them, and they'll understand because they love me very much.

I already love my church,
I love my church very much; I give five bucks every week to the church's renovation fund because I want a beautiful place to pray; but when the usher seats me next to you-know-who, I get so upset and cuss him out under my breath, and forget to pray, and tell everyone after the service—and they all smile because they love me very much.

I already love my country,
I love my country very much; I'd die for my country; and when its time to pay my taxes,

> I get very insulted,
> I kick up a storm,
> I clench my fist and vow a fight to the finish;

and then I

> reconsider, and
> pay my taxes, and
> fudge only a little

because I know my country will go to war over me because she loves me very much.

I already love myself,
I love myself very much, so therefore I make absolutely
sure I'm first in everything, and first everyplace I go.

I love myself very much—so much so that all my wants
and pleasures will be satisfied:

I love
>>my junk foods,
>>my cigarettes,
>>my liquor,
>>my sugar,
>>my fats,
>>my salts,
>>my pills,
>>my drugs,
>>my sex;
and then I'll get sick and blame everything on
>>God,
>>family,
>>neighbor,
>>church,
>>country,
but never myself because I love myself very much.

It is then that *that* word "love" should take
>>a break,
>>a day off,
>>a long vacation because it has been
>>so overused,
>>so overworked,
>>so overdone because it isn't meaning what
>>>it's saying anymore.

Perhaps the only way to truly love God
              with all our hearts,
              with all our soul,
              with all our mind,
              with all our strength—and our neighbor
                  as ourselves—
is to be like my good friend Michael. When only five
years old, Little Michael was asked to show how much he
loved his Uncle Louie. Michael
              immediately,
              joyfully,
              spontaneously
extended his two hands completely behind his back and
stretched them as far back as they could possibly go and
said with a large smile, "That much!"

෯

In my understanding of children, a five-year-old child is
without the capacity of manipulating love in a way adults
sometimes do. God wants all of us to be like a five-
year-old child: innocent in pure love to one another.
When we are, we truly *love* God and neighbor.

10 Changing Water to Wine

2nd Sunday of Ordinary Time (C)   John 2:1-12

You heard them cursing, "Jesus! Jesus Christ! He's changing water to wine, he's changing water to wine! Christ Almighty!"

Jesus changed the water to wine.

Today, if anyone changed water to wine it would be a
really big news story:

> "Hold the presses,"
> "Here's the scoop,"
> "Read all 'bout it."

It would make the front pages of every newspaper in
every town and city on the face of the globe. It would
be one of those media extravaganzas that brings

> TV anchorpeople and reporters,
> radio commentators and analysts,
> syndicated columnists and journalists

to ask those god-awful silly questions:

> "How did it feel?"
> "Were you aware what was happening?"
> "What did you do to prepare?"

The media hype would then center on the *what else:*

> Can he change a stale brownie into a scrumptious homemade double-layer strawberry short cake?
>
> Can he change a worn-torn ten-dollar bill into a newly printed thousand-dollar bill?
>
> Can he change a badly dented 1969 Ford into a 1989 solid gold Rolls-Royce?
>
> Can he change a plain, dowdy, usual-looking brunette into a sensuous blonde?

In Jesus' time, all this hot-air speculation would have been contrary to the mission he was embarking on. Jesus was consistent in his efforts not to overwhelm God's love by his miraculous power. Jesus wanted his miracles to show forth, to illuminate the new age he was bringing from God to his Father's people.

John, the fourth scripture writer, had the same idea. John's

> first sign,
> first miracle

of Jesus was to say to believers

> that the *word* is now *flesh,*
> that the *light* is now *life,*
> that the *Messiah* is now *here,*
> that the new *epoch* has *begun,*
> that the *Son* is really *God.*

John made sure it was in the context of a celebration. What other celebration can be more significant than a wedding reception?

More than any other celebration, a wedding feast denotes

> the beginning of new life,
> the promise of more life,
> the expectation of many life miracles.

Somehow those many life miracles have become ho-hum
encounters:
>we've gotten used to miracles,
>we've even gotten bored of miracles,
>we've been missing too many miracles of
>life.
At least those people who saw Jesus change water to wine
began cursing in their excitement,
>they couldn't contain their ebullience,
>they recognized a miracle for what it was.

I saw a movie the other night, *A Soldier's Story.* The film
was about a black captain-lawyer in the army during
World War II investigating the death of a black sergeant
in a small Louisiana town. Upon arriving at the army
base, the black officer was met with a great deal of skep-
ticism by fellow white officers. In the end, however, the
lawyer brought immense credibility to his mission of justice. The white captain offered the black lawyer a ride to
his destination as a fitting tribute for a job well done.
The white officer said to the black officer (and I
paraphrase), "I guess I have to get use to black officers
now?" The response was a predictable, "Guess you have
to get use to black officers now."

I tell that story because it was
>a miracle of accomplishment,
>a miracle of recognition,
>a miracle of respect and admiration.

Many times
>a black woman,
>a yellow man,
>a red boy,
>a white girl
are not considered miracles no matter what they accomplish.

Many times pregnancies are not considered miracles and life is not allow to continue.

Many times talents and gifts are not considered miracles and they are ignored.

Many times age and wisdom are not considered miracles and they are forgotten.

Many times the world in all its beauty is not considered a miracles and missiles are stored in silos ready for destruction.

Many times the ability
             to alter,
             to adapt,
             to amend,
             to change
is not taken seriously and
             miracles become commonplace,
             miracles become tiresome,
even extinct.

11 God's Great Covenant with the Poor

3rd Sunday of Ordinary Time (C)   **Luke 4:14-21**

When Jesus unrolled the scroll and proclaimed the Isaiah
passage, the passage that refers to the poor,

> The Spirit of the Lord is upon me,
> because he has anointed me
> to bring glad tidings to the poor.
> He has sent me to proclaim liberty to captives
> and recovery of sight to the blind,
> to let the oppressed go free,
> and to proclaim a year acceptable to the Lord,

he was actually reaffirming
> an honest-to-God pact,
> a bond,
> a Covenant God with the poor of this
> world.

We live in a fast-paced world,
> a world where zillions of business transac-
> tions are conducted over the phone dai-
> ly for billions of dollars;

a world where thousands of multi-
national corporations are investing billions of dollars for expansion and
profit weekly;
a world where hundreds of conglomerates are wheeling and dealing for a mil-
lion new customers annually.

And yet, for all that, we still live in a slow-paced world,
a world where millions face extermina-
tion for want of food and housing;
a world where billions exist in the filth of
poverty, disease, and exploitation;
a world where millions are denied the
freedom and liberty the Creator so
desired.

The other day I wondered if the "haves" of our world,
who seem to be doing things right and who believe that
God is on their side, have ever told the "have nots" of
this world that God is *equally* on *their* side?

Jesus, by proclaiming Isaiah's words, wanted to reassure
those neglected by home or society that God has given
the Word to them that *their God* is indeed on their side.

I found it interesting that Jesus reaffirmed God's promise
to the poor in a house of worship. It is in synagogues and
churches that these words are expounded. Unfortunately, however, communications from these houses of God
to the poor are many times feeble at best. Many of the
poor fail to receive
the covenant,
the hope,
the joy,
and instead they are
displaced,
unwanted, or
ignored.

The other night I had a dream. I dreamed I died and went to heaven. As I was walking up the narrow dirt road that leads to the Kingdom of God, I saw the figures of four people by a newly painted picket fence, the kind of fence one would expect to see in Mark Twain's *Tom Sawyer*. The four people all died the same day—the day I succumbed. As I came closer, I recognized each of them. They were dedicated people with whom I had association. The four were praising one another for their accomplishments, patting each other on the back. As I joined them by the fence, they welcomed me with open arms.

It was at that time that a beautiful light shone and our eyes gazed straight at it. The light was soothing—unlike any other light ever experienced on earth. It was God. After God's brief introduction to us, the Almighty apologized for not personally directing us to the Kingdom but that Jesus would accompany us momentarily.

Each of them then began telling of their accomplishments that certified them to enter the Kingdom of God. The first person boastfully uttered, "I invented books. Without me and my superior intellect, people would have remained in the dark. I kept people's interests alive, their minds clear, their bodies active. I even allowed for people's fantasies to become real:

> they met many wonderful and intriguing people of centuries past;
> they traveled the world over, every sensational and exotic hide-away;
> they feasted on the most delicious and appetizing food earth could offer."

The second person proudly spoke, "I invented paper. Without my cleverness and artistic ability, books would never have been a reality. But with my invention, money

had become my greatest art. With money, I gave people
>   new hopes,
>   new lives,
>   real future.

My invention caused governments to listen, politicians to
dance, churches to take notice, and caused people to do
anything."

The third stated dramatically, "I invented pens. Without
my invention, people would have been without words to
write on paper and print in books. But with my in-
genuity and entrepreneurship, people became owners of
their feelings. I was responsible for people expressing love
to one another who normally would have found that
hard to do in the spoken word. Because of me, people became
>   lyricists,
>   ethicists,
>   philosophers,
>   dreamers,
>   poets,
>   storytellers."

The fourth, in his usual lofty style, cited, "I invented ink!
Without my discovery, the people of the world would
have been in disarray. Though there may have been
books, paper, and even pens, all would have been to no
avail without my ink. But because of me, people began
believing one another:
>   contracts were signed,
>   statements documented,
>   policies endorsed,
>   doctrines recorded,
>   treaties witnessed, and then,
>   peace was proclaimed."

When finished, we looked around and unknown to us all, Jesus had been there during the entire conversation. The Master was pleased to hear of the dedicated service we had all achieved while on earth. Jesus extending his hands toward us and said with a smile, "I want to escort all of you into the *kingdom,* but just step aside for only a few minutes because I see John (John Palmer) coming up the road.

Now John was a street person of years past. John had a problem with alcohol:

> John drank—and walked the streets,
> he drank—and asked for coffee and a
> sandwich,
> he drank—and asked for shoes now and
> then,
> he drank—and was a mess most of the
> time,
> he drank—and drank for forty years or
> more.

Then one very hot summer day John asked for *water* and, after quenching his thirst, thanked God for the water.

Jesus met John halfway to the picket fence and took him by the hand and walked him through the gate of the fence while the others followed behind.

This is what is meant when God made *the Covenant* with the poor: they will enter the Kingdom of God before all those who keep saying,

> "I",
> "I",
> "I".

12 Sending the Seventy-two on a Mission of Joy

14th Sunday of Ordinary Time (C)   Luke 10:1-12,17-20

Have any of us ever been in a situation of ministering to the need of people, where we ought to feel the presence of joy, only to feel a disruptive, internal feeling of gloom—even of self-pity?

At those times it seems misery grabs us, holds us, and leads us to the way of nowhere. What, then, challenges us to see our situation more clearly? In this particular case, a fly.

> At a moment,
> on a street,
> in a place,
> two hundred homeless people *visualized.*

> All alone,
> in a back room,
> isolated from everyone,
> an obsession *materialized.*

Chopping onions, carrots, potatoes,
slicing tomatoes, radishes, cucumbers,
baking meatloaf,
the mission of bread *actualized.*

Radio blaring,
93 degrees, 95% humidity,
pores open,
sweat *vaporized.*

A fly,
intruding upon the kitchen,
harassing a mere mortal,
human eyes observing—'tention, eyes *par-
ticularized.*

The insect buzzing,
over head,
near ear,
battle plan *conceptualized.*

Fly stalking,
mortal eyes fixed,
waiting: right moment,
human hand moves,
slowly,
deliberately,
swat!
missed, *demoralized.*

Again, fly hovers,
human eyes glaring,
hand positioned,
steady,
strike!
Wham!
A *hit! Capitalized.*

In the greasy water,
among sudsy pots,
fly lands,
alive,
barely;
mortal *tranquilized.*

Atop mucky water, fly
cannot fly,
fightin' to safety,
seekin' freedom,
nearin' edge,
bug *traumatized.*

Oops, water from mortal hands,
pours over wounded pest,
brought to middle again,
insect begins anew the struggle for life,
situation *dramatized.*

Five minutes elapsed,
then ten,
now twenty,
water bombardment cleverly *finalized.*

Moral annoyance turns to delight,
control!
power!
power!
power!
Power over a fly!
Creature *terrorized.*

Mortal comes to senses,
leaves,
life has far greater possibilities,
this now *factualized.*

༆

You see, the fly fought to live for whatever life meant to it, while the person in this story wallowed in disarray, missing, in part, the extraordinary privilege of service to neighbor by the very call of God. This calling to discipleship is offered to each of us by our Creator. So let us not be distracted from free and joyful service—or else a challenge will come our way; but in turn, this challenge will keep us from being

> *immobilized* and
> *paralyzed* when the mission has to be
> *realized.*

O Loving One: grant to all of us who strive for discipleship your joyful presence so that our service may always be just, plentiful, and love-filled. Amen.

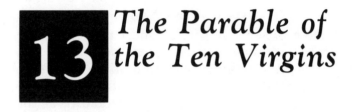

13 The Parable of the Ten Virgins

32nd Sunday of Ordinary Time (A)   Matthew 25:1-13

Been on a trip lately?

If you're anything like me, the planning for your trip was
              extensive and complete;
              nothing overlooked,
              nothing left to chance.
Everything for your trip was gone over with a fine tooth
comb:
              the front door repaired,
              new luggage bought,
              spigots turned off,
              paper girl alerted,
              paychecks cashed,
              travelers' cheques purchased,
              car tuned-up, gassed, and oiled,
              road maps picked up, and
              Aunt Katie alerted to the time of your ex-
                  pected arrival.

Nothing is left to chance and preparations go smoothly, without a hitch.

Somehow, unfortunately,
> no matter how meticulous we have been,
> no matter how organized we are,

a flaw appears, in an instant, that unravels it all:
> an important item forgotten,
> an essential detail overlooked.

When I was thirteen, my parents and I traveled to the Poconos for our annual vacation. It was the hottest July I can recall. Upon arriving at our cabin, in unison we remembered our dog, Buttons, was left behind, alone, without water and food. Moreover, no one would be at the house to let Buttons out. My dad drove back a hundred miles to "retrieve" our pet so that our vacation would escape further disasters.

There was another time when three college roommates and I decided to take a trip to California. The four of us planned for a good month. We explored all the possible question marks, hoping to avoid any mishap to secure a successful summer vacation:
> where to go,
> where to eat,
> where to stop,
> where to sleep,
> what to visit,
> what route,
> who's car,
> who's driving,
> how long,
> how fast,
> the cost.

As we were approaching Idaho, a couple days after starting out, it dawned on one of my roommates that he was missing all his keys. His keys were important because we were given a house in Colorado to stay for a week, and the house key was among the missing set. He decided to call the college library where he last remembered having them. After a frantic search, the keys were located, locked in his car in the library's parking lot!

My most chaotic experience, however, occurred the winter of '78. I was leaving the big city on my way to a seminary in a little town outside Allentown, Pennsylvania, called Center Valley.

My friend and I arrived at the train station with plenty of time to spare. As we were chatting at the station, I double-checked the arrival and the departure times of my train, the Allentown express. I also double-checked the track number. My luggage consisted of two badly mutilated suitcases, which were packed to the hilt, and two supermarket-type boxes of books. My friend was helping, carrying the latter.

Everything seemed correct; everyone was confident all was under control. The announcement was made, "The Allentown express will be leaving in five minutes." My friend and I felt no great urge to scramble about because the track was in front of our eyes. We leisurely walked to the track and boarded luggage and myself on to the train. Once aboard the train, my friend shook my hand, wishing me "Good luck and Godspeed," when all of a sudden he shrieked, "The train's heading to Baltimore!"

The train jerked with a momentary pause, as if ready to pull out full strength, and that was my signal to get off mighty fast. I threw my two suitcases down to my friend and jumped off as the train started picking up speed. The books
   forgotten,
   lost forever.

From this moment on any semblance of order went out
of order:
>
> holdin' one suitcase, my buddy the other;
> scoldin'
>> "thataway" the conductor points, and
>> "thataway" we dart;

Flo at the info desk fingers
> "downaway" and
> "downaway" we flow;

"No, no," the porter hems,
> "upaway" and
> "upaway" we gallop;

"Hold, hold," a passenger says,
> "aroundthataway" and
> "aroundthataway" we barrel on.

"Holy Moses, No! It's to Paoli and to Yardley; to Valley
Forge and Jenkintown—it's not Allentown!" we chime.

Across the ramp we putter; the Colonial Special to Boston is off and sputtering.

In the restroom we recover and discover the shoeshine lad
had the gall to pick up the ball, "The Allentown express
is off the wall."

> In the haste,
> train movin' with grace,
> suitcase breaks,
> all my goods rollin' without grace.

On the platform lay:
> the sprays,
> the roll-ons,
> the pants,

the shirts,
the socks,
the underwear,
all my all!

❧

The purpose of these three stories is to illustrate that human planning is not without flaws.

What Jesus is indicating to all of us in the parable of the ten virgins is the need to go beyond human preparation when seeking the Kingdom of Heaven. Jesus is reminding all of us to invest our trust into his care unconditionally, so that we can be truly prepared for his coming again.

14 "I Have Come Not to Abolish (The Law)"

6th Sunday of Ordinary Time (A)   Matthew 5:17-37

"What is Real?" asked the Rabbit...
    "Real isn't how you are made," said the Skin Horse. "It's a thing that happens to you. When a child loves you a long, long time, not just to play with, but *really* loves you, then you become Real."
    "Does it hurt?" asked the Rabbit.
    "Sometimes," said the Skin Horse..."When you are Real you don't mind being hurt...But those things don't matter at all continued the Skin Horse , because once you are Real, you can't be ugly, except to people who don't understand"

Realness,
            not make-believe,
            not a reasonable facsimile, but Realness.

Realness is what Jesus wants from all of us.

Not long ago, while shopping at one of the major department stores, I accidentally bumped into a mannequin and knocked it to the floor. I quickly stooped and picked up the mannequin, and though I was

in haste to honor a luncheon commitment, it seemed as if
time simply stood still,
> my breathing took a long pause,
> my foot became glued to the floor,
for there, before my very eyes, stood the mannequin as
Real as fake can be.

What was curious about
> this sensuous piece of art, rather,
> this piece of plaster and plastic,
was the alluring presence her face had upon me. And because of that presence, my initial embarrassment of even
thinking for a split moment that it was Real evaporated.

> The mannequin's eyes: the brightest of
> blue and most delicate;
> the eyelids: compelling to vulnerable and
> expressive;
> the eyelash: a soft pink;
> the lips: orange-touched;
> the brows: heavy and arched;
> the blush: worn high on the cheekbone,
> adding warmth;
> the petite nose: accentuating the natural-
> shaped chin;
> the jawbone: taut and firm;
> the natural reddish hair: glamorous and
> stylish in its sophisticated permanent
> wave look.

When I returned to the Real world and regained my
perspective, I pardoned myself to the dummy and continued my shopping.

As I left the store, I had a hearty laugh thinking how silly
of me for taking a mannequin for Real.

Seeing mannequins in department stores and knowing they're not Real, except as a novel approach for selling merchandise, is a unique reminder of the gift of life that I have been given and of the enjoyment in sharing my life with others.

Now while Jesus was about his mission in Galilee, he was noticing the many people who resembled mannequins. Many of the people Jesus encountered

> looked stiff and motionless;
> seemed spiritless and lifeless;
> appeared not to be *really real* though they
>   were Real.

This outraged the Master.

Then one day, as Jesus entered the synagogue to pray, as was his daily custom, a young man was standing in the aisle offering prayers to Yahweh. But the man was not communicating his feelings to his God. Jesus, sensing this, felt sadness; it was as if the man's

> heart,
> soul, and
> life

were inanimate objects totally distinct from his body.

Jesus approached the man, noticing as he did the deep crevices and dark shadows of a beleaguered face; the many wrinkles and droopy chin betrayed a tired and burdened life long before its time;

> the eyes sluggish and bloodshot, and
> the lids weary and dull, denoting a life of
>   misery and submission;
> the lips limp and crackly, cheeks drawn,
> the grayish-pale indicating a lack of fel-
>   lowship and humor.

Jesus, moved by compassion, gently placed his hand on the man's cheek, and a smile appeared. It was the first time the man smiled in many years.

The leaders of the synagogue observed all that was transpiring and decided to confront Jesus.

The chief priest asked, "Are you the Mr. Jesus we have been hearing so much about?"

"I suppose," answered Jesus.

The chief priest then stated, "Our membership drive has been over for a while now; we have to ask you to leave the premise immediately. You are too much for us to bear."

"What are you *really* telling me?" inquired the Master.

The charge against Jesus came forth from the mouth of the insolent leader, *"You are real, too real,* for us; you have broken too many of our most sacred laws. So leave, will you!"

"What laws have I broken?" insisted Jesus.

The chief priest replied quickly, "We have a list of charges that is as long as the day:

> *You have touched people:*
> you touched a paraplegic, lifted him from
> his wheelchair to go near the beach—
> *and it was a Sunday!*
> You ate lunch with a prostitute—and
> had the gall to have dinner with
> a *homosexual!* How dare you?!
> You are *forgiving* too many people; we *do not* have to forgive our enemy. And
> do you not know there are *limits!?*
> You are a *wimp:*
> you *pitied* the 5000—and fed them;
> you *cried* over a dead man—and they said
> you did *magic!*
> you *wept* for Jerusalem—but Jerusalem is
> *still* here;
> you *value*

dumb people,
deaf people,
blind people,
old people,
executives, even
welfare people!

You are not fasting,
you are not purifying,
you are just hanging around with
    trouble-makers who have absolutely
    no education, and
you are *loving them!*

And above everything else, we under-
    stand you are calling God your *daddy!*

We cannot have this,
we have a respected institution;
we are not about to have you making
    people *real.*

Do you understand, Mr. Jesus?"

Jesus focused his eyes directly on all the religious around
him and angrily retorted:
        "I do understand, but
        I do not understand. My Father
            created everyone,
            loves everyone,
            allows everyone the freedom to be
            Real.

        But you have circumvented the Law to
        suit your own purposes and made slaves
        out of my people. And you call it religion.

You have made my people ugly and un-
  Real;
you have made my people into mannequins.

I am leaving now, but I will be back
shortly—and when I come back, I will
resurrect the Law. I did not come for a
funeral, I came for *life—life* that is *real*,
with people who are *real!*"

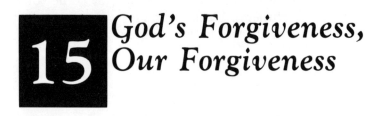 God's Forgiveness, Our Forgiveness

---

11th Sunday of Ordinary Time   Luke 7:36-50

Being a writer of sorts, I am never without my
"whiteout," the ink eraser of our sophisticated age. What
I do with "whiteout" is, whenever I make a mistake writ-
ing my stories, be it
> spelling,
>
> a wrong word or two, or
>
> the wrong punctuation,

I simply take
> my correction fluid,
>
> my "whiteout,"

and dab it over the mistake and let it dry. When it dries,
which takes only a few seconds, this enables me to continue my thoughts as though the error never occurred.
Indeed, when doing this procedure, a
> wonderful,
>
> exhilarating

feeling warms me knowing I have the power to right
something wrong that appeared on a piece of paper.

When I matured in my storytelling proficiency and dared use the

> most-advanced,
> most-modern,
> most-up-to-date

typewriter and typed at will in the church's office, I was pleasantly surprised and thankful to find and master the automatic backspace correction key, the typewriter's equivalent to "whiteout." In a jiffy my mistakes were

> blotted out,
> taken away,
> covered over,
> forgotten, and
> gone forever.

I was

> free then to continue plotting my stories,
> free to explore the dimensions of my mind,
> free to prod life's experiences,
> free to continue the challenge to perfection,
> free from error, knowing my "whiteout" was always at hand.

It occurs to me that we fragile people

> fall into the temptation,
> fall into the trap, into the rut of whiting out
> our mistakes,
> our failures,
> our imperfections, indeed
> our sinfulness
> without being introspective,
> without being honest with ourselves.

We rush to our
    shops,
    stores,
    counters
and buy gallons of "whiteout" and
    rub,
    dab,
    smooth it over ourselves and thus
    absolve ourselves of everything and
    forget,
    ignore,
    thumb our noses at the
    mistakes,
    faults,
    sinfulness
of our neighbors and hide our left-over supply
    for another time,
    for our sole use.

Thank God
    God is not like that!
    God doesn't hide the "whiteout"!
    God gives "whiteout" to everyone, an un-
     limited supply to all!
    God in the past whited-out the failures of
     so many.

Take David for example, his wrongs ranged from
    pride to
    sex—with someone's wife, to
    murder (the husband of the wife), to
    hypocrisy.

Then God,
thank God, sent the prophet Nathan
    to whiteout David's past,
    to renew David. David

> realized the need to forego the past and
> accepted the challenge of introspection,
> accepted the pardon offered by God.

One day

> God saw the need to whiteout people's
> sins forever, so
> God sent Jesus to whiteout people's sins
> eternally.

When Jesus appeared some wanted to experience his whiteout, but many others were snubby and refused.

Take Simon, for example,

> Simon the Pharisee.
> Simon was a
> delightful,
> smiling,
> exciting,
> easy-going sort of guy,

the kind of fellow one would feel comfortable around. Simon

> was always throwing parties,
> was truly the life of any party.

Simon threw a party for Jesus. He wanted preferential treatment from the "prophet." Simon always received preferential treatment wherever he went, for he was a respected civic and church leader. And Jesus indeed wanted so much to give Simon preferential treatment.

When so many people were calling Jesus a "prophet," Simon just had to have him over his house—so that the news would spread

> all over town,
> throughout the country-side.

This for Simon would be the icing on the cake: Simon would become a much sought-after dinner speaker.

At the party however, a woman known to be a sinner came to Jesus:

> she didn't call him a prophet—she sensed he wasn't that formal;
>
> she didn't really speak to him—she saw in his eyes his spirit;
>
> she cried—she knew she needed him, so much so she wanted to change her ways—
>
> something Simon never thought of,
>
> something Simon cared not to think of,
>
> something Simon dared not entertain—

because he was so wonderful just as he was, and besides everyone liked his smile and were used to him now and really enjoyed having him around. "So why change?" Simon thought. Much to Simon's consternation, it was the sinner who got the preferential treatment from Jesus; she knew forgiveness and was able to love others in return.

> Simon knew no forgiveness and was only able to love himself, if one calls that love;
>
> Simon *did* know how to whiteout his mistakes—only to lose paradise in the process.

16 "The Kingdom of God Is Like a Mustard Seed"

11th Sunday of Ordinary Time (B)   Mark 4:26-34

The kingdom of God is like a mustard seed. When it is sown, it is the smallest of all the seeds on the earth. But once it is sown, it springs up and becomes the largest of plants.

Hum, hum. Like to break in on you, Jesus.

Sure.

I know what you are telling the crowd, but it doesn't ring a bell with me. I don't want to be selfish. I know there are many grieving people. But Mister, heal
>   my pain
>   my struggle
>   my fragileness
>   in my world,
>   in my heart, now!

The reign of God you talk about seems
>   far away, so
>   far off.
Do you really expect us to believe you?

Can you, Mister, address my need to be healed today?

Tell me your pain. I do care. I want to be near you. Give me your hand.

> Lost my job.
> In debt.
> Rent is due.
> No food.
> Feel powerless.

I am sorry. I feel your helplessness. Go ahead and cry, no need to feel embarrassed.

I've been

> ridiculed,
> humiliated,
> rejected.

I know the misery. I remember feeling just like you. Let me hold you—soothe your pain.

I feel useless, unwanted. All alone.

You have me. I

> *need you,*
> *care for you,*
> *love you.*

You don't know

> my pain!
> My pain is hurting me!

Give me your pain. Surrender it. It's all right to yell.

I'm not only in pain, but ugly too!

You are beautiful.

No I'm not!

Marvelous creation you are. I mean that. I love you—even if I did not, you are still beautiful.

Doesn't help my pain!

Give me all your pain.

Don't know how.

> *I want to hug you.*
> *I want you to feel my*
>   *love,*
>   *tenderness,*
>   *strength.*

I lost someone close. I am
          lost.
          Rejected.
          Unsure.

Your hurt must be unbearable. I will
          never lose you,
          never reject you.
I need you too much. I love you too much.

Why are you crying, Jesus?

Because you are crying, my friend.

But why are you crying?!

You do not believe I really love you.

My struggles are killing me, Jesus! Life stinks. I need to be
understood!

Life is a struggle. Let me carry your load.

Why?

You are good, and you are hurting. Do you believe that you are
good?

I don't know.

So many people need you, love you. Look around, friend. Open
your eyes. People need you, your love: there is

a crippled lady,
a person with cancer,
a lonely grandmother,
a teenage boy on drugs,
a smiling group of high-schoolers,
a young fatherless boy,
an oppressed woman,
a depressed neighbor,
an eager senior citizens group,
a battered wife,
an abused child,
a divorced mother,
a group of people needing a prayer leader,
a young woman addicted to alcohol,
an unfulfilled grandfather,
a bereaved father,
a happy group of elementary children.

They all

need you,
need your love!

But I

don't love myself,
don't even *like* myself!

Why not?

I'm not acceptable.

To whom?

Myself. Others.

I accept you. So does my Father who
formed you,
molded you,
loves you!
Should you not love yourself?

I'm in too much pain for that!

My friend, now I am in pain!

Why?

Because you are. Put your arms around me. I need
your tenderness,
your strength.

I will care for you, Jesus, give you tenderness, strength. I
love you despite the pain. Oh, it's still there, deep inside,
and will be for a while. It's okay now, you've cared for
me. I know love. I have experienced myself in you. I chose
to
like myself,
love myself!
Because I now know I am loved. I choose to love others in
the same way, Jesus.

Why are you crying now?

I see a future, I have gone beyond my present, the reign of
God is
here and
beyond.

❧

The Kingdom of God is like a person who had pain, the
greatest of all human frailty, yet once experiencing total
love, grew to become a whole person able to inspire
others to become.

17 *Jesus Is Tempted by Satan*

1st Sunday of Lent (A)　　　　　　　**Matthew 4:1-11**

In the barren desert in the Middle East stands a shrub that has withstood the test of time and weather. This shrub has seen and heard the comings and goings of so many events and people. It has been said that this shrub has stood there since the beginning of creation, and that more than anyone, it knows the sound of God's voice: its gentleness and its thunderous fury. This shrub is silent, its feelings hidden in a vault inside its small trunk.

One day, while the shrub was soaking in the bright rays of the sun in the Garden of Eden, God planted an immense department store in the middle of the garden for the convenience of humanity's first couple, Adam and Eve. God carefully explained to Adam and Eve that they could select any merchandise in the store except the chocolate-covered cherries laying on the counter. God reiterated: "All is yours, the
　　　　　TVs,
　　　　　stereos,
　　　　　air conditioners,

> refrigerators,
> cars,
> boats,
> minks,
> dinning room sets,
> jewelry,

but do not eat the chocolate-covered cherries laying on the counter." God's voice was more explicit, "If you eat the chocolate-covered cherries, you will surely become ill." Both Adam and Eve acknowledged God's command as they left for the store.

The shrub was shocked to see old man Satan disguised as a check-out person at the great department store. As Eve was leaving the store with many fine articles, Satan told this gullible girl that she would have more knowledge than the voice whose face was hidden and who made everything from nothing if she would only eat the chocolate-covered cherries. "Oh, I shouldn't," Eve replied to Satan.

Suddenly Eve was overwhelmed with envy and lust for prestige and power, and, when no one was looking, Eve quickly took the chocolate-covered cherries from the counter and ate them without thinking of the consequence. After having her fill, Eve insisted Adam have his share of the cherries. Soon after, both of them became violently ill and

> very,
> very human.

Old man Satan could be heard laughing as God's voice shook the earth in condemnation as the pair left the garden. Yes, old man Satan had begun his campaign of deceit and trickery; naturally, the shrub was furious.

Years later, Cain and Abel were working in their father's gas station when, lurking behind the shrub, old man Satan started plotting his next move. Because of Cain's lack of self-esteem, he was easy prey for Satan, who disguised himself this time as a bartender.

Cain, incidentally, was at odds with his brother because Abel spent much time in prayer, dialoguing with a voice that wasn't visible. "Laughable," Cain would often rebuke Abel, citing the nonsense of a God in a voice who prefers listening to people more than anything else. As time went along, Cain became more and more incensed with Abel's closeness to an invisible God, hoping to frustrate his brother's attempt to seek out that voice.

Then one evening, while Cain was driving Abel in the family pickup truck through town to pick up supplies, Satan took hold of Cain's senses. "Let's stop at this bar for a couple drinks, Abel," said Cain, knowing the consequences of several shots of whiskey and mugs of beer.

After five hours of continual drinking, Cain, being inebriated, left the establishment with his brother. On the way home, Cain failed to negotiate a right turn, crashing the truck into a concrete wall and killing Abel. Cain escaped unhurt. God's voice was heavy in outrage; far away from the scene, the howling laughter of old man Satan was heard. The shrub, feeling totally powerless to do anything, began to cry.

God's voice was silent for a long time thereafter until one day, many centuries later, old man Satan, breathing easier, felt it was safe for him to come out of hiding. This insidious creature disguised himself as a fellow traveler, hoping to meet Jesus in the desert.

It so happened Jesus met old man Satan face to face on a cool, breezy day. As Jesus was walking and praying to that voice he called "Abba," it enraged old man Satan. This sly devil knew he could do to Jesus—and to all humanity—what he did to Eve and Cain.

Old man Satan had a proposal for Jesus: "If that voice is your daddy, order that voice to turn all these stones
> into silver dollars,
> into stocks and bonds,
> into diamonds and gold,
> into plain old *money!*"

Jesus quickly answered him, "People need more than
> money,
> securities, and
> medals
to live."

Then old man Satan took Jesus to the edge of the mountain and showed him all the cities of the world:
> Tokyo,
> Bombay,
> New York,
> Moscow,
> Rome,
> London,
> Paris,
> Beijing,
> Cairo,
> Istanbul,
and told Jesus they would be his if he would acknowledge him instead of the voice that really didn't exist.

Jesus reiterated, "Only my Father deserves such honor."

Finally, old man Satan told Jesus: "I will make you
> President of the United States,
> Premier of the Soviet Union, and
> Emperor of the entire Universe
in one instant if you will only pay me homage."

Jesus bitterly retorted, "Get out of my sight, you old fool!"

With that, the cool breeze that had been blowing around intensified and became a swirling gust of wind that knocked old man Satan flat on his duff. Old man Satan scrambled to his feet and fled in fright while Jesus felt comfort and reassurance in the wind he called "Abba."

The shrub rejoiced in happiness, for when it saw the face of Jesus, it also knew the voice it longed to see.

18 *The Card Player*

27th Sunday of Ordinary Time (A): Respect Life Sunday

When I was younger, I enjoyed playing cards. I was intrigued by the way people played a game of chance. I was enthralled by the mighty egos of many card players, for they seemed to be actually playing themselves rather than the cards. I watched the facial expressions and body language of these players in order to guess their next move. I observed intensely to see what card they would play and to try to understand the reasons why they hadn't used the same suit or the same card against their opponents that I might have.

Of all the card games I watched and played, I enjoyed Poker best of all. I became *that* player that I had watched for so long!

I remember a hand—the most unforgettable hand I had ever seen. There were seven of us playing poker. We were playing for big stakes; in fact, we had to show one thousand dollars to join the game! We had been playing for quite a while, some forty hours or more, and we were all getting tired. Suddenly, *the* hand appeared! It was the last poker game of the night, five-card draw, and, as was our custom, the last game was pot limit.

The first person threw three cards into the discard pile in order to receive three more from the dealer. The second player did the same. The third player threw away two cards, as did the fourth player. The fifth player threw in only one card, hoping to draw an inside straight. The sixth player took the limit anyone could take: four cards. The dealer stood pat.

The betting began, and each player upped the ante of the player before, until the dealer with the pat hand took charge and upped the ante an incredible $200.00, one hundred dollars *more* than all the others. It was allowed because, as I said, it was pot limit. The dealer was trying to scare everyone out of the game so that he could win it all—even without showing his hand!

The first player, named "Nervous Tom," who had opened the ante, sat nervously for a few tense moments and then decided to show his openers and drop out of the game. The second player, "Calm Mike," a peaceful sort of guy, totally unbaffled by the bump, matched the $200 and upped the ante yet another $200. The third player, "Old Dan," the oldest one of the bunch, folded without any hesitation. The fourth player, "Baby-face Georgie," threw in his $400 somewhat reluctantly. The fifth player, "Carl the Bum," as he was fondly called, folded—not because his hand wasn't good, but because he was low on money and the rent was due! The sixth player, "Louie the Loser," was scared—he very seldom won anything and he knew he wasn't going to win this one. The dealer, "Johnny, the Wheeler-Dealer," saw all the raises and decided to up the ante to $500. With this, "Calm Mike" backed off and dropped out without even a murmur; while "Baby Face Georgie" hung in for all that it was worth; he matched the pot and even boldly challenged "Johnny, the Wheeler-Dealer," to an incredible $1000 raise! To my knowledge, the game is *still* going on...

꙳

You see, the poker game is the game of life and each player is being knocked out of the game by those who, like "Johnny, the Wheeler-Dealer," see no reason why they should share the same gift of life equally.

The first player to fold was "Nervous Tom," who symbolizes all those who are profoundly retarded or emotionally unstable. The second player to fold was "Old Dan," who symbolizes the elderly in our society, most especially those who just manage to survive in their homes or in nursing homes. The third player to fold was "Carl the Bum," as he was fondly called; he symbolizes those street people who are on our streets, nowhere to go, dead ends everywhere. He also represents those without income, those who are unemployed or who are being squeezed in our economic vice. The fourth player to fold was "Louie the Loser," for he represents the criminals who are stored away in our many warehouses and whose lives are expendable. The fifth player to bow out was "Calm Mike," who symbolizes peace rather than war; who symbolizes a better world if nations could calmly understand the destructive nature of missiles, bombs, and guns. Finally, the sixth player, "Baby Face Georgie"—he's still playing, still fighting—for he symbolizes the unborn.

Now, in this game of life, where are *we* going to throw our chips?

19 *Corpus Christi*

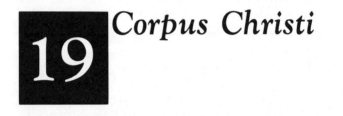

10th Sunday of Ordinary Time (B)   Mark 14:12-16,22-26

"This is a CBS News Special Report." We all know how that sounds. We wait in eagerness for the bulletin that is about to be sprung on us. Well the news the other day sounded just like that: "This is a CBS News Special Report: Jesus Christ has just announced he would like all people to reform themselves. In a prepared speech delivered in Jerusalem, the Son of God called on all people to transform themselves into his likeness. Stay tuned to CBS News for further details."

That's impossible. Who the heck does he think we are that we can be like him?

> We're only human—can't he see that?
> We're not super people—doesn't he
>   know that?
> We're not computers—doesn't he have
>   enough common sense?
> We're not perfect—he should know that
>   already; he's been around long enough.

But it seems Jesus is not going to take "no" for an answer. He's going to continue to burden us with demands to be like him.

To be like him means feeding people. We cannot do that, especially when we're laid off from our jobs after years of hard work and good service, only to be asked to feed bums who never worked a day in their lives. How dare they come to us! Feed them? You've got to be kidding. No way! Absolutely not!

To be like him means caring for people. We cannot do that, especially all those people who talk about us behind our backs, who discredit us everywhere they go, who tell lies about us. Care for them? Good grief, no! No way! Absolutely not!

To be like him means forgiving people. We cannot do that, especially that auto mechanic down at the gas station who charged us $348.00 when the whole job cost $72.00. Forgive that thief? Oh God, no! No way! Absolutely not!

To be like Jesus also means to accept fellowship meals with all kinds of people: the sinners as well as the saints. This means breaking bread with the bum we wouldn't feed; this means breaking bread with that person who talks about us; and this means breaking bread with that auto mechanic who robbed us.

And when we do share our bread with one another at the table that is rounded it may be
>   white bread,
>   wheat bread,
>   rye bread,

corn bread,
spoon bread,
shortening bread.
Any of these breads give us the essential
vitamins,
proteins, and
minerals
necessary for life.

When Jesus shares a fellowship meal with us all, all of us who are saints and sinners, Jesus offers special bread that only he can give—he gives himself.

And when Jesus gives himself to all of us and we accept, we then have the extraordinary power to reform our lives.

It is in reforming our lives that we all receive the awesome gift of eternal life.

"This has been a CBS News Special Report."

ॐ

When using the word "bum," I exaggerate a popular expression I heard when growing up in Philadelphia. I am sure and hope we have a more sophisticated expression today that recognizes the dignity of all God's people.

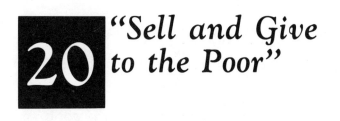

20 "Sell and Give to the Poor"

28th Sunday of Ordinary Time (B)   **Mark 10:17-30**

God created; what God creates, God treasures and loves. Now what may not be as well known is the fact that God tolerates even the bad of his people-creation. God tolerates the bad because the Creator fully expects and genuinely hopes for a change for the good. Now this is not in keeping with the Almighty's perfection—being God, God should know better. But God cannot help it. God

> enjoys,
> relishes,
> delights,

in the fullness of people-creation.

God loves both the good and bad, or in keeping with more contemporary jargon, God loves the winners and losers of people-creation. God loves the winners and losers because the Almighty never knows what to expect in return for the gift of benevolence and supreme love.

More than anything else, God loves surprises. God loves surprises especially when losers turn their lives around and become winners. However, the other side of the coin is: despite the love God has for surprises, the Creator feels very badly when winners turn their lives back and become losers.

>Lucifer was such a winner-turned-loser, and so were
>the Pharaohs of ancient Egypt,
>King Nebuchadnezzar,
>Rich man who couldn't part with his wealth,
>Judas, to be sure,
>Nero, who wanted to rule the world, and
>a host of others.

But when a loser becomes a winner,
>God rejoices,
>angels and saints sing, and
>good people everywhere celebrate.

There were
>David of Israel,
>Dismus of Calvary,
>Saul of Tarsus,
>Augustine of Hippo,
>Frances of Assisi,
>Nobel of Geneva, and
>a host of others.

I'd like to tell you a story of a particular day that not only surprised God but also made the Holy One's day more joyful somewhere in heaven. It was a day when two losers did what was needed to be done, and both of them became winners because of it.

It happened the day before Christmas Eve in a large and very cold prison cell, where two young men were to meet one another. Both had been arrested earlier in the day and both had undergone the dehumanizing and humiliating procedures of imprisonment.

These two men came from totally different directions in life and in understanding. One sat in a chair, all alone, crying uncontrollably in self-pity; the other also sat in a chair with six others in another corner of the cell.

The one by himself was white; the other was black, as were the other six with him. All of them had
> their rights stripped,
> their nakedness exposed,
> their very personhood infringed upon.

Even though they were united by these injustices, neither cast eyes in the other's direction. Acknowledging people whose skin color was different was not acceptable behavior in their individual communities. Fear, suspicion, even loathing was the spoken and accepted law.

Finally the young black man could no longer ignore the younger white man, who was not bearing his burden too well. The black man approached the fellow and offered consoling and supportive assurances. The black man gave the white man hope for the future; his wisdom gave the white man the ability to see beyond the present crises, and his wisdom gave shape to a better and more profound vision
> of himself,
> of life, and
> of all people.
In that one instant they both became winners.

The white man left the prison three days later while the black man remained behind bars. I believe that neither were ever the same again.

Even the nobodies of this world can give hope and love to the poor of this world. The poor of this world can give hope and life to the rich of this world or to anyone willing to be challenged to accept God's *people-creation!*

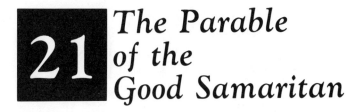

The Parable
of the
Good Samaritan

15th Sunday of Ordinary Time (C)   **Luke 10:25-37**

> Injustice is injustice is injustice.
> Injustice to anyone is injustice to
>   everyone.
> Injustice is an insult to God,
>   an affront to God's grace,
>   an assault to personhood,
>   an inexcusable sin.

I've always looked upon injustice done to another human being as injustice that ought to be righted no matter what the cost.

A Samaritan is up the road a bit; he has injustice painted all over him—a non-citizen in a land called promise.

A Jew, his face smeared with blood and injustice, lies face-down in a ditch on the side of the road—a victim of violence in the promised land.

The Jew is left for dead after being
          stripped,
          beaten, and
          robbed.
"Someone help! Help me!" he cries.

A priest, traveling the same road, sees the injustice done
to another; he feels sorry for his compatriot, but
nevertheless mumbles to himself, "I would like to help
the poor soul, but mustn't touch or I'll be
defiled—anyway justice
          is justice
          is justice
and justice at this moment is honoring Yahweh at the
Temple." In his haste to avoid touching the victim, the
priest's foot unknowingly steps on the man's hand in the
land of promise.

Not long afterward, a Levite spots the mangled body,
which is seemingly grasping for its final swallow of air.
Being a Temple caretaker and an ardent observer of the
Law, the Levite stands near the body and distinguishes
between justice and injustice. He concludes, "God
deserves what is due him, and that is ultimate justice."
Already twenty minutes late for the Temple sacrifice, he
sidesteps the body, offering as he did a muffled blessing
of sorts, "Where is there justice in our land of promise?"
The Levite continues on his way, unknowingly kicking
the man's foot. He feels justified knowing justice
          is justice
          is justice.

The Samaritan,
the outcast,
the despised,
the one who is the living symbol of embarrassment in this land of promise,
notices the
injustice that is
unjust that wasn't
just done to a fellow human being. He feels compassion.

The Samaritan stops; he doesn't ask himself, "What does the Law require? What should I do?"

The Samaritan walks toward the gentleman; he doesn't ask him,
"Are you a Jew?"
"Are you an Arab?
"Are you a Republican?"

The Samaritan stoops over the man; he doesn't ask,
"Do you have insurance?"
"Do you have Blue Cross?"
"Do you have AAA?"

The Samaritan kneels over the body; he doesn't say, "Checked my calendar, don't have a free day till next week, so hang in there."

The Samaritan holds the person's head on his lap; he doesn't say, "My checking account funds are low, hope you're alive next payday."

The Samaritan wipes the stranger's face; he doesn't say, "I have a painting job for you when you get well, then we'll be even."

The Samaritan bandages the wounded traveler; he doesn't say, "Need your address, the bill will be in the mail."

The Samaritan takes the pilgrim to the nearby inn; he doesn't say, "The motel up the road is too expensive—it's a matter of principle, you understand."

> The Samaritan did what he had to do.
> The Samaritan had compassion.
> The Samaritan knew justice.

Jesus told his parable to alert the lawyer to answer his own question and challenged the lawyer

> to see beyond preconceived notions,
> to think beyond confining laws,
> to go beyond age-old biases,
> to love beyond the immediate neighbor.

When I think of this parable, I reflect on the many people who are today

> living,
> lying, even
> dying in ditches (imaginary ditches to the
>   outsider, real ditches to the victim),
> seeking compassion because of someone's
>   injustice.

These people are

> battered,
> bewildered,

seeking assistance from

> someone,
> anyone,
> a stranger,
> a Samaritan.

People do come passing by the ditch. Their names are

> family,
> friends,
> neighbors,

> co-workers,
> associates,
> strangers.

They know justice as well as the Samaritan.

They make distinctions between right and wrong, but so often they would rather
> walk by injustice instead of
> defend justice.

They at times offer transparent assistance with
> paternal,
> maternal
blessings of sorts:
> "How unfortunate."
> "It's a damn shame."
> "Isn't it a pity."
> "...and to such a nice person."

They are unwilling to soil their hands to save the person, even the spirit of the person, lying
> in the ditch
> in this land of promise.

Without realizing it, people who ignore others in bad times in effect
> step on,
> kick the dignity out of the human person.

Observe, if you will, the injustices that may (and *will*) put people in ditches in the coming weeks.

> Injustice is injustice is injustice.
> Injustice to anyone is injustice to
> everyone.

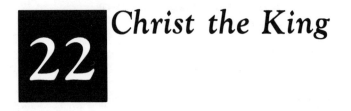

Christ the King

22

34th Sunday of Ordinary Time (B)   John 18:33-37

At one time or another we have all dreamed of being *king*
or *queen*
> of our neighborhood,
> of our street, even
> of our homes.

We dreamed if only, if only we had
> all that authority,
> all the glitter that goes with it,
> all the bowing that's part of it,
who knows what kind of leader we would be? Who
knows what kind of command would dare come from
our mouths? We
> may act very powerful,
> might do very stubborn things, or
> could act very pompous—
but when we awake and realize being a king or queen is
only a dream, we go about our daily routine, knowing the

unreality of it all. And being very rational, we are thus satisfied that the only way of being king or queen was through a dream.

Yet, do you know there are people who
        never let go of that dream,
        pursue that dream?
        hound that dream? Always trying to
        catch that ever elusive dream?

Pilate was such a guy. He always wanted to be king. And because he wasn't, Pilate was one person in all scripture who didn't love himself. Most of the more infamous characters in the Good Book had trouble loving themselves *too* much—but not Pilate.

Pilate was procurator (governor) of all Judea, but he wasn't satisfied; he wanted to be
        king,
        king for a day,
        king for a lifetime.

We might think that, being procurator, Pilate was a rather secure sort of gent, but he wasn't; he was not only insecure but frustrated as well. Pilate's insecurity made him increasingly jealous and ruthless, which detracted from his governance of Judea. For Pilate, becoming king was taking all so long;
        he wanted to be king quickly,
        he wanted to be king
            for a day,
            for a lifetime.

At the same time in Galilee, Herod was another
        insecure,
        frustrated,
        elusive dreamer.

Herod was tetrarch, a sort of prince, but he too wasn't satisfied. He dreamed of being

> emperor,
> emperor of the entire world,
> emperor
>> for a day,
>> for a lifetime.

Herod was in a duel with Pilate to gain prominence in Rome, where the real power resided.

Then one day the people brought the "king of the Jews" before Pilate, charging him with blasphemy for all the gentle and beautiful things he said and did on his travels.

The ambitious procurator stood in front of this "king." Pilate was furious for he had dreamed about being called "king," and no one was calling him "your majesty."

The more Pilate mocked the "king" and his attire, the more he wanted to be king; and the more he wanted to be king, the more he took his frustrations out on the "king of the Jews." The more Pilate took his frustrations out on the "king," the more questions came out of his mouth:

> "What have you done to deserve being called king?"
> "How many armies have you conquered?"
> "How vast is your territory?"
> "How much money have you sent to Caesar?"
> "How great is your wealth?"

Jesus answered, "I only conquer hearts."

Pilate

> laughed,
> cursed, and
> dismissed the "king."

Pilate wished to share his laugh with Herod, hoping Herod would respond to his initiative, and hoping someday to become king. So Pilate sent the "king" to Herod.

Herod gladly accepted Pilate's offer. He had heard about this "king" and he was anxious to see him.

Herod
>>> had a good time,
>>> had a grand time,
couldn't stop laughing, managing only a few words:
>>> He's not a king!
>>> He's not even an impostor!
>>> He's contemptible—get him out of here!

Herod sent the "king" back to Pilate with warmest regards. Neither recognized the "king" as being a king, but both of them recognized each other for being what they were—and they became friends forevermore.

23 Sermon on the Mount

All Saints' Day   **Matthew 5:1-12**

Have you ever noticed the many things we do on a mountain?

I remember when I was five years old, playing with someone's fire truck and pretending to be a fireman, fighting a blaze from atop a small, stone hill. I was a whiz at avoiding those stones that were blocking my engine and keeping me from my date with destiny. Then I got older.

When I was not quite seven, I used to run up and down a dirt hill that, to me, was the biggest mountain I had ever seen. I had fun wrestling with my friends and sliding down the mountain, making big dirt clouds and watching them float and fade into the sky, hoping that someday my dreams would also reach the sky. Then I got older.

When I reached my tenth birthday, I was the marble champion of the orphanage. My friends and I would play atop a concrete hill. We played for

the biggest,
the brightest,
the most mysterious marbles.

I was the happiest, the proudest when I collected all the cat-eyes to be had. I had achieved something, but I knew there were other and more important things to accomplish in life. Then I got older.

When I was fourteen, I took my first train ride to a mountain in upstate Pennsylvania. It was the first time I saw a real, live mountain—and I was disappointed. I realized, for the first time in my life, that my mountains of

hills,
stones,
dirt, and
concrete

were not the real things. I also realized that mountains were not the fun and adventurous things of my youth:

fighting to the last man, defending my
Alamo,
blowing soap bubbles to the sky and
watching them burst,
making images from the passing clouds
high up there.

Now I realized that mountains were serious business for all concerned with serving the public good:

there was a hydroelectric plant operated
by the public utility;
there were poles and wires owned by the
telephone company;
there was a huge antenna owned by the
local television company;
there were lights to guide airplanes to a
nearby airport;

there was a tunnel through the mountain, erected by the state for the
tourists;

there were also stores, cabins, and cable
cars operated by the Chamber of
Commerce; and

there was a military site that was govern-
ment private property—

and rumor had it that nuclear missiles were hidden there.

Well, Jesus gave hope to many people from atop a mountain; he spoke of compassion and love

not only to the electric company of his
time,

not only to the Ma Bell of his time,

not only to the media of his time,

not only to the giant conglomerates of his
time,

not only to the Chamber of Commerce of
his time,

not only to the United States Govern-
ment of his time,

no, Jesus spoke not solely to the powerful and mighty,
not solely to the prestigious and influential, Jesus spoke
directly

to the poor,

to the hungry,

to the suffering,

to the abused, and

to the peacemakers as well.

When Jesus spoke with them, he didn't hide his feelings;
Jesus was upfront, honest, and loving.

Today, however, we hear of another mountain: the
mountain of rational thinking. Today we hear "I did it
on my own, so they can also climb the mountain on their
own." And in so doing we somehow ignore the Sermon
on the Mount.

The Sermon on the Mount has become optional, for there are other things to be done on the mountain. Many people climb their own mountains and find fault with others who cannot.

> We lay blame and continue climbing our own mountain.
>
> We sometimes point fingers and accuse, deny equal treatment to others, and then allow stones from under our feet to fall on top of others while climbing the mountain.
>
> We often enjoy engaging in innuendoes and mud-slinging at others' expense as they begin to falter and we continue climbing the mountain.
>
> We at times find it easy to believe derogatory statements about our neighbors, even willing to cast rocks of our own as we continue climbing the mountain.
>
> We frequently defame reputation while the boulders we heave damage another's life while we continue climbing the mountain.
>
> We say...
> We say...
> We say...

It's a shame we get older.

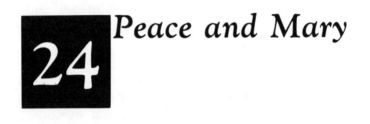

24 Peace and Mary

New Year's Day   **Luke 2:16-21**

As we all know, January 1st is not only the beginning of a
new year, but it is also the day
> we propose,
> we make,
> we begin

resolutions that will guide us through this year in peace
and happiness and on to the next year to meet more challenges in good shape and fashion. We say things like:
> "I'm going on a diet and sticking to it."
> "I'm not going to spend one penny over
> my budget."
> "I'm going to be more assertive and gain
> that promotion."
> "I'm not going to be rude to anyone."
> "I'm going to do better in school and do
> more homework."

We also know our resolutions usually last as long as
children's Christmas toys: about two weeks into the new
year.

However, the most
>>> thought-about,
>>> hoped-about,
>>> talked-about
resolution from time immemorial the world over is peace:
>>> genuine peace,
>>> durable peace,
>>> lasting peace,
>>> individual peace and comfort,
>>> family peace and security,
>>> world peace and mutual understanding.

But it seems the year is not a week old when Bob loses his job at Brown and Williamson and Susan is laid off from Hercules, and financial worries begin to drain the family's resolve and savings.

It seems the year is not a month old when the burdens of life give way to
>>> despair,
>>> anxiety,
>>> depression.

At these critical junctions of our lives, it may be of help for us to give pause to the lesson of Mary, whom we heard in today's gospel text treasuring and reflecting all that was revealed.

Our overview of Mary in years past has been one
>>> of peace and serenity,
>>> of acceptance and compliance,
>>> of perseverance and determination.

But the truth is, Luke, as most scripture writers, was a storyteller. Storytellers of scripture try to give insights into the marvels of the God with us and how gradual these insights comes.

Mary in actuality is like all of us: given to
                unscheduled,
                unrehearsed,
                uncommon circumstances.

When we hear of Mary—and in scripture it is not all that often—we sense the gravity of her relationship to God:

The angel announced to Mary that God is going to dwell in her womb, "Oh God, O my God!
                I'm not ready,
                I'm not prepared,
                I'm only
                      a peasant,
                      a pauper.
Why on earth is God coming to my neighborhood—and what does God want with me?!" After several minutes of angelic explanation, Mary continued with a puzzled look, "If it's alright with God, its OK with me."

Later, Mary visited Elizabeth,
                "God has found favor with me,
                God wants me to give birth to a son—his
                      son!
Furthermore, the angel said the child must be born in Bethlehem. I don't understand." Mary paused, then continued, her voice upbeat, "I'm going to get the best room in the best hotel for him 'cause he's God—and only the best for God! But what will Joseph say when he learns I'm pregnant?"

And when the best hotel in Bethlehem was filled, and when the lights were dimmed at the Best Western Motel and various travel lodges booked, Mary in her confusion found a room
                in a burned-out building,
                in the lower part of town.

And Mary invited all the strangers passing by to see
              her God,
              my God,
              our God.

When Jesus was twelve and Mary and Joseph were
searching for him for a few days, they found him in the
Temple, and Mary questioned her son. "Woman," he
answered her, "I've got to be about my Father's mission."

"Woman?!" she replied.
              Oh God,
              my God,
I'm your mother, don't you understand?"

When Jesus began his public ministry, the whole family
was at a party, a wedding reception, and
              the booze had run out,
              the beer keg gone dry,
              the wine flattened out,
and Mary approached her son, "What can you do to save
this party?" And Jesus replied, "Woman, what business
is it of mine?"

"Woman?!" Mary responded.
              "Oh God,
              my God,
I'm your mother, can't you understand?"

When
              the public whisper,
              the public talk,
              the public scandal
around town was about
              her troublemaking son,
              her possessed son,
Mary went to see him near the lake where he was having a
meeting with his disciples behind closed doors. Someone

opened the door and there she stood, and Mary heard, "Who is
> my mother?
> my brother?

Only those who follow my Father's will." Mary spoke, "Come with me, son, before they kill you." No reply came forth, so Mary spoke,
> "Oh God,
> my God,

I don't understand."

It was when Mary saw her son on the cross giving up his life that she cried,
> "Oh God,
> my God,

now I understand.
> I am your servant.
> I will follow you."

25 The Meaning of Easter

2nd Sunday of Easter (B)   **A Reflection**

The other morning I wondered why
            this Easter season,
            any Easter season,
is so holy and special.

And while I was praying and reflecting by the sea, I thought about my best friend, Michael, who died nine months ago. I realized all the more he wasn't around this Easter time. Only thirty-six years of age. And why?

Mike is buried, and grass is growing atop the plot;
April arrived, and a blizzard is forecast;
Jesus said, "unless you become like children, you will not enter the Kingdom";
I'm getting ready to plant my vegetable garden in the backyard with last years' decomposed pumpkin;
Our country has destructive nuclear missiles capable of destroying the Soviet Union forty times over named, of all things, "the peacemaker."

            Contradictions,
            Inconsistencies,
            Conflicts:

We meet a lot of them in our lives; our days are full of them. They can easily become roadblocks and, if we are not careful, entangle our efforts to find

> stability,
> consistency, and
> peace.

But when roadblocks come, as they surely will, are we going to deal with them? Or will we try everything to avoid those roadblocks, as if they're figments of our imagination, and call for the trash collectors?

The trash collectors come with their trucks and they take

> all our garbage,
> all our trash,
>> our problems,
>> our struggles,
> all our pain,

and grind them into microscopic particles and take them to a dumping site the other part of the state where they all get buried. All our concerns are disposed of inside a hole, tucked neatly away inside our planet.

> It is however from that hole that hopes arise;
> it is in the dying that life arises.

Do we believe it?

There is a newspaper company in my home state that uses only recycled paper to print tomorrow's news. It saves on the ecology of the world we inhabit. It makes a little town, far away, a more beautiful place to live instead of the wind using so much time and energy moving paper

> from street to street,
> from block to block.

What a paradox! Last year's news becomes today's news.

As I look at the recycled newspaper I see the death of old news but

> life to new news,
> life to new hopes,
> life to new horizons,
> life to dreams that people before me failed
>   to achieve.

> Old/New
> Destructive/Peaceful
> Garbage/Vegetable
> Adult/Child
> Snow/Sun
> Death/Life

These are all daily reminders that death is never death.

Mike is dead, but I got news the other day from, of all people, his children (ages 12 and 9 respectively), informing me his sister Donna gave birth to a baby girl, Christina. And then I got to thinking: what a fascinating God we have! While God was taking Michael home, God was actually giving Michael's family another human being

> to hold,
> to treasure,
> to love.

The lesson of Michael is that hope

> lives,
> arises

in death. And that is why God rose Jesus from the dead.

In Jesus' resurrection we have the ultimate hope—and that is why

> this Easter season,
> any Easter season,

is so holy and special!

❧

The idea for this reflection came from an article entitled "Paradoxes: composting and empty tombs," written by Mary Beth Lind and appearing in the magazine *The Other Side.*